*Double Dip*

*Egret*

*Flip flops*

*Inquirer & Mirror*

The Inquirer and Mirror
NANTUCKET'S NEWSPAPER SINCE 1831

*Jeep*

*Nantucket flag*

*Oversand Vehicle Permit*

*Pail and shovel*

*Scallop*

*Turtle*

*Xmas*

*Yarn*

*Zschock*

 *Arbor*

 *Bass*

*Cranberry Scoop*

*Gardiner's Corner*

*Hydrangea*

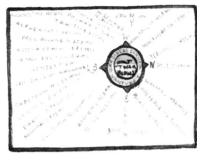 *Kite*

*Lobster*

*Mermaid*

*Quail*

*Rosa Ragusa*

 *Umbrellas*

 *Victory*

*Weathervane*

# Journey Around

# Nantucket

## from A to Z

Martha Day Zschock

COMMONWEALTH EDITIONS

*Beverly, Massachusetts*

ISBN-13: 978-1-933212-82-1

Commonwealth Editions is an imprint of Memoirs Unlimited, Inc.,
266 Cabot Street, Beverly, Massachusetts 01915.
Visit Commonwealth Editions on the Web at www.commonwealtheditions.com.

Visit Martha Zschock at www.journeyaround.com,
or stop by journeyaround.blogspot.com for current updates, fun facts,
interesting tidbits, and enjoyable journeys!

10 9 8 7 6 5 4 3 2 1

Printed in Korea

*To my wonderful family,*

*And to happy Nantucket memories.*

*Special thanks to the supportive folks at Commonwealth Editions
and to Allison Carter for her fact-checking help.*

*"Never forget your summertimes, my dears."*

—STUART LITTLE

# Greetings, my friends, and
# Welcome to Nantucket!

LOCATED ALMOST THIRTY MILES OFF THE COAST OF CAPE COD, the small island of Nantucket has captured the hearts and imaginations of folks from around the world. Its history and future are closely tied to the sea that surrounds it.

Fondly known as "The Grey Lady," Nantucket is the only place in America that is an island, a town, and a county all with the same name. Formed by a glacier, the island was home to Wampanoag Indians for thousands of years before English captain Bartholomew Gosnold mapped it in 1602. Other European settlers soon followed, and finding the island unsuitable for farming, they turned their attention to raising sheep and to whaling. As a busy whaling port, the town bustled with candle factories, ropewalks, sail lofts, and other maritime businesses. In the twenty-first century, with whaling long gone, Nantucket remains an international port of call for tourists and summer residents, and the island has a vibrant year-round community that is proud of its heritage.

There is much to explore, so come, let's take a journey around Nantucket!

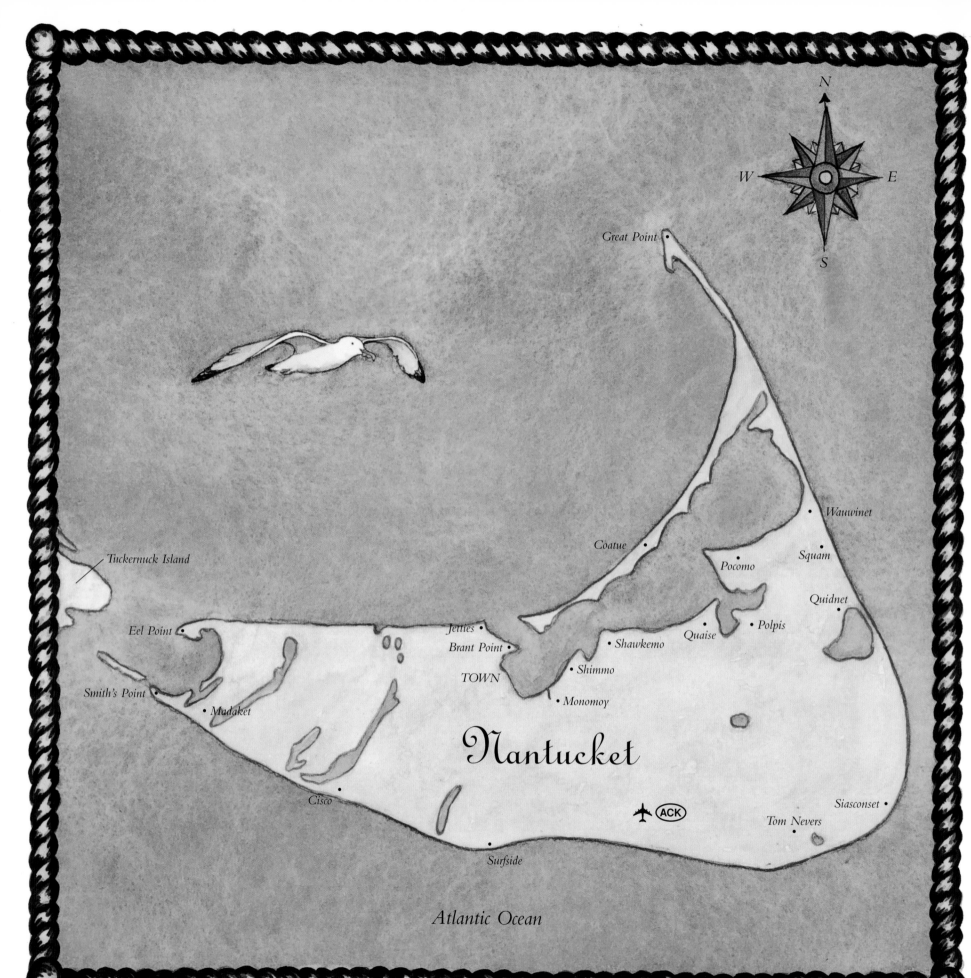

Away in the Atlantic, an island awaits.

CAPE COD

MARTHA'S VINEYARD

NANTUCKET

WAMPANOAGS, NANTUCKET'S FIRST INHABITANTS, gave the island its name, which means "faraway land." Their legends tell of the giant Maushop who created Nantucket with sand from his moccasins. As English settlers arrived, they brought with them diseases that proved fatal to the native population. Many island locations have maintained their native names: Polpis (Branching Cove), Siasconset (Place of Bones), and Monomoy (Black Soil) are a few.

For a safe return to Nantucket, toss two pennies overboard as you sail around Brant Point!

Main: Welcome to Nantucket
Inset: Wampanoag artifacts, Whaling Museum
Detail: Brant Point

Beacons and blasts warn boats: "Beware!"

BEFORE MODERN NAVIGATION DEVICES, Nantucket's three lighthouses—Brant Point, Great Point, and Sankaty Head—played a critical role in safeguarding vessels. Flashing lights and horn blasts guided sailors around the island's treacherous shoals and through frequent fog. Weathering storms, erosion, and fire, the beloved landmarks have been rebuilt, relocated, and strengthened to ensure that their comforting lights will continue to shine for future generations.

Main: Brant Point Light
Inset: Fresnel Lens, Whaling Museum
Detail: Sankaty Head Light

Sankaty Head Light's viewing platform was widened in 1856 to accommodate ladies' hoop skirts!

Crimson cranberries carpet conservation acres.

Sand

Peat

Gravel

Clay

THE HEALTH BENEFITS OF CRANBERRIES have long been recognized. Native Americans combined them with deer meat to make pemmican, an energizing snack, and sailors ate them to prevent scurvy. First cultivated by Cape Cod's Capt. Henry Hall in 1816, cranberries soon became important to Nantucket's economy. With 234 acres, Nantucket's cranberry bog was once the world's largest. Today 40 acres are cultivated under the Nantucket Conservation Foundation.

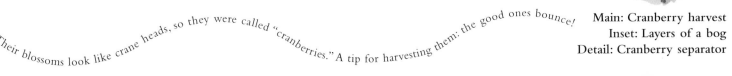

Their blossoms look like crane heads, so they were called "cranberries." A tip for harvesting them: the good ones bounce!

**Main:** Cranberry harvest
**Inset:** Layers of a bog
**Detail:** Cranberry separator

**D**eer don't devour daffodils.

WHEN SUMMER RESIDENT JEAN MACAUSLAND learned that deer shared her passion for tulips, she began a campaign to plant daffodils across the island instead. Since 1974, residents and garden club members have continued the plantings and look forward to an annual display of over 3 million blossoms! The Daffodil Festival celebrates the arrival of spring with an antique car parade, tailgate picnics, contests, and lots of fun!

Main: Daffodil Festival parade
Inset: Picnic
Detail: Daffodil varieties

Garden club members help local schoolchildren grow bulbs for the flower show.

Daffodils come in a variety of sizes, shapes and colors.

E rosion eats away at the earth.

POUNDING WAVES AND STRONG WINDS erode beaches during storms. When seas are calm, gentle waves gradually rebuild the shoreline, a process called accretion. About a half-mile of Nantucket's southern and eastern beaches has been lost since colonial times. Precariously perched near the bluff, Sankaty Head Light was moved four hundred feet to a safer location. Unfortunately for seaside homeowners, most efforts to deter erosion have not proved successful.

Don't step on the beach grass. Its intricate root network helps prevent erosion.

**Main: Sankaty Head Light**
**Inset: Effects of erosion**
**Detail: Dune**

**F**olks flock from ferries.

IN THE LATE 1800s, tourists began discovering Nantucket. Large hotels were built, and summer boarders were welcomed to island homes. Steamers brought visitors to the island, and a small train provided round-trip service between Surfside and Siasconset for thirty-five cents. Today, Nantucket's airport and ferries make getting here easy, and tourism is the island's leading industry. In the summer, Nantucket's population swells by 500 percent!

Main: Arrival
Inset: A remnant of Nantucket's RR, The Club Car
Detail: Come fly with me!

After Boston, Nantucket has the second busiest passenger airport in Massachusetts. Its code is ACK.

ACK

Great
wealth
grew from
greasy luck.

FROM THE EARLY 1700S TO THE MID-1800S, Nantucket prospered as whaling capital of the world. In hopes of "greasy luck," a ship loaded with valuable whale oil used in lamps and candles, whalers tracked slow-moving right whales near shore, then searched the world for prized sperm whales. The island's economy revolved around the whaling industry, and many women ran businesses while their husbands were at sea.

Returning captains displayed pineapples to say guests were welcome. The pineapple remains a symbol of hospitality.

**Main: The Three Bricks**
**Inset: Petticoat Row, Centre Street**
**Detail: Pineapple**

# Horseshoe House held happy hearts.

THE OLDEST HOUSE ON NANTUCKET was built in 1686 as a wedding gift for Jethro Coffin and Mary Gardner; her family gave the land and his family donated the timbers. The marriage reconciled the two families, who had argued about the island's government. The upside-down horseshoe on the chimney symbolically held their love together. In 1987, the house underwent a major restoration after being severely damaged by lightning.

Main: Oldest House, Sunset Hill
Inset: Oldest House hearth
Detail: Oldest House kitchen garden

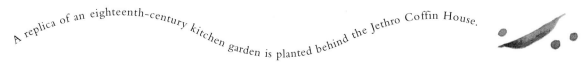

A replica of an eighteenth-century kitchen garden is planted behind the Jethro Coffin House.

Idle hours
Initiated
intricate art.

ABOARD LIGHTSHIPS FOR MONTHS at a time, crewmen eased boredom by weaving baskets to sell on shore. Woven around a wooden mold, the cane baskets evolved over time as others carried on the tradition. Coveted by collectors, many are now worth thousands of dollars! Shipwrecks southeast of Nantucket prompted creation of the Nantucket South Shoals Lightship Station in 1854. To sailors, such lightships were considered "Guardian Angels of the North Atlantic."

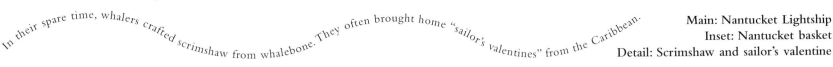

In their spare time, whalers crafted scrimshaw from whalebone. They often brought home "sailor's valentines" from the Caribbean.

Main: Nantucket Lightship
Inset: Nantucket basket
Detail: Scrimshaw and sailor's valentine

# Journey to Jetties for the Fourth of July!

WITH SO MANY GREAT BEACHES on Nantucket, it's hard to choose a favorite! Young children prefer the calm waters and fun activities on the island's north shore, while the more adventurous flock to the surf along the island's south side. Wide expanses of calmer surf line the more remote eastern coast. Nantucket's beaches are beautiful, fragile, and mostly privately owned. Please stay on designated paths and help clean up trash.

**Main:** Jetties Beach
**Inset:** Sunset at Madaket
**Detail:** Summer fun

Jetties Beach celebrates July 4th with fireworks. Beachgoers also look forward to a day for sand castles.

K ilns fire kids' creativity.

IN 1945, ARTISTS FORMED the Artists Association of Nantucket and opened the island's first art gallery. Soon after, Old South Wharf became a center for artists, who established studios and galleries in former fishing shanties. The Artists Association and the Nantucket Island School of Design and the Arts, located in a converted dairy barn in Wauwinet, offer a variety of classes for kids, who experiment with paint, clay, and natural objects.

The Theatre Workshop of Nantucket offers children's performances and drama camps.
Celebrities are often spotted at the Nantucket Film Festival.

Main: Old South Wharf galleries
Inset: Artists Association of Nantucket and NISDA
Detail: Autograph please!

# Launch a Lure and land some luck!

ABUNDANT FISHING AND SCALLOPING GROUNDS have always provided a living for islanders and excitement for anglers. The season for Nantucket's big four—striped bass, bluefish, bonito, and false albacore—begins in May. Once thought poisonous by locals, Nantucket Bay scallops are now considered among the best in the world. If you're on the water and smell watermelon, toss in your line: It's a sign that bluefish are nearby!

Main: Great Point
Inset: Nantucket's famous scallops
Detail: The Haul Over

Fisherman once dragged their boats across the "Haul Over," a path in the narrow dunes used as a shortcut to fishing grounds.

**M**eet on Main, meander through town.

FOLLOWING WORLD WAR II, Nantucket's wharves and buildings were in disrepair. To preserve the island, developer Walter Beinecke Jr. stepped in, buying and restoring most of downtown. Fancy shops opened, attracting tourists. Beinecke set aside conservation land and donated funds to spruce up island landmarks. Lost to a storm a century earlier, the First Congregational Church's steeple was replaced in 1968. Climb up ninety-four steps to see the spectacular view!

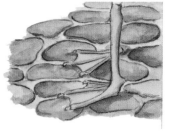

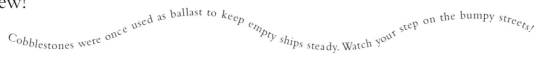

Cobblestones were once used as ballast to keep empty ships steady. Watch your step on the bumpy streets!

**Main:** Main Street
**Inset:** First Congregational Church
**Detail:** Downtown cobblestones

# Newtown became known as New Guinea.

**BLACK HISTORY TRAIL**

1. Whaling Museum
2. Dreamland Theater
3. Antheneum
4. Unitarian Church
5. Sherburne House
6. Anna Gardner's House
7. "Colored" Cemetery
8. Five Corners
9. African Meeting House
10. Florence Higginbotham House

NANTUCKET ABOLISHED SLAVERY IN 1773, ten years before the rest of Massachusetts. African Americans worked as tradespeople, laborers, farmers, and whalers. Many free blacks built houses near the Old Mill, forming their own community. Newtown Gate separated their neighborhood, called New Guinea after their African roots, from the white community. Recently restored as a museum, the African Meeting House was once a school, meeting house, and church.

**Main:** African Meeting House, York Street
**Inset:** African American History Trail
**Detail:** A+ kids

Denied admission to school because of her race, Eunice Ross fought for desegregation in 1847.

O bserve with open eyes.

*Observe with open eyes.*

NANTUCKET'S ATHENEUM has served as the island's library and cultural center since 1834. On a clear October night in 1847, Maria Mitchell, an astronomer, educator, and the Atheneum's first librarian, discovered a comet with her telescope. She became famous for her observation and was awarded a gold medal by the king of Denmark. During her life, she fought against slavery and promoted women's rights.

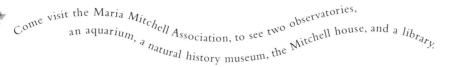

*Come visit the Maria Mitchell Association, to see two observatories, an aquarium, a natural history museum, the Mitchell house, and a library.*

Main: Maria Mitchell House, Vestal Street
Inset: Atheneum, India Street
Detail: Loines Observatory and MMA Aquarium

P aved paths provide pleasurable pedaling.

CLIFF

MADAKET

FAIRGROUNDS ROAD

DIONIS

'SCONSET

EEL PT.

POLPIS

OLD SOUTH ROAD

SURFSIDE

NANTUCKET'S SMALL SIZE (14 miles long and 3 miles wide), its flatness, and its beautiful scenery make it the perfect place for biking. And you'll avoid the traffic! The island has over 24 miles of paved paths that can take you from town to 'Sconset, Madaket, Eel Point, and more, while color-coded signs point you in the right direction.

In a former lifesaving station, Nantucket's youth hostel is a perfect resting place for biking vacationers.

Main: Bike path, Polpis Road
Inset: Bike path signs
Detail: Star of the Sea Hostel

**Q**uaker beliefs shaped Nantucket's culture.

-let her receive encouragement for the proper cultivation of her powers so that she may enter profitably into the active business of life

- Lucretia Mott -
1793~1880

A ✕ B ✕ C

DURING THE 1700S, half of all Nantucketers belonged to the Society of Friends, and Quaker beliefs strongly influenced island culture. Simplicity reigned; even for wealthy families, houses and clothing styles were quite plain. Believing that the spirit of God exists in everyone, Quakers encouraged education for girls and opposed slavery. Nantucket women and African Americans thus had improved opportunities.

Quakerism declined in the 1800s; houses became more ornate; and William Hadwen's grand home, built in 1845, shocked locals!

Main: **Quaker Meeting House, Fair Street**
Inset: **Sampler**
Detail: **Hadwen House, Main Street**

# Rambling roses rise to the roofs.

SCONSET, SHORT FOR SIASCONSET, is seven miles from downtown, but feels worlds away. Settled as a whaling outpost in the seventeenth century, the village has many quaint cottages that were once fishing shanties. In the early 1900s the area became a popular summer spot for city folks. A bustling arts community followed, with many Broadway stars performing at the Casino—which never was used for gambling, despite its name.

Main: "Auld Lang Syne," Sconset
Inset: Sundial
Detail: Chanticleer

Actress Agnes Everett opened the Chanticleer in the early 1900s as a tearoom serving ice cream cones—a novelty in those days!

# Surfmen saved sailors shipwrecked on shoals.

## Heroic Rescue!

January 20, 1892. Battling gale force winds, Captain Chase and his six man crew at the Coskata Life Saving Station heroically rescued all seven men aboard the H.P. Kirkham that struck the dreaded Rose and Crown Shoal 15 miles off Great Point. The brave mission lasted over 24 hours. The ship, laden with salt and pickled fish was bound for New York from Halifax, Nova Scotia. It sank within an hour of the rescue, its cargo lost to the sea. Captain

HUNDREDS OF SHIPWRECKS OCCURRED along Nantucket's shoreline. "You have to go out, but you don't have to come back" was the motto of the courageous U.S. Life-Saving Service. Patrolling beaches, they organized crews to pull survivors ashore using breeches buoys and surfboats. The Egan Maritime Foundation and Nantucket Life-Saving Museum preserve their heroic tales.

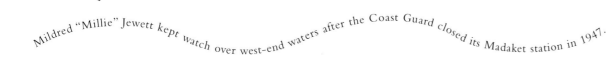

Mildred "Millie" Jewett kept watch over west-end waters after the Coast Guard closed its Madaket station in 1947.

Main: Nantucket Life-Saving Museum
Inset: Hear Ye! Hear Ye!
Detail: Millie's House, Madaket

Throughout time, turbines have turned.

BUILT IN 1746, AMERICA'S OLDEST continually operating windmill, the Old Mill, harnessed wind power to grind corn. Global warming has made renewable energy sources imperative, and Cape Wind proposes to build the country's first offshore wind farm in Nantucket Sound. It would generate 75 percent of the Cape and islands' electricity. The project is hotly debated; opponents fear it will spoil the area's natural beauty.

Main: Old Mill
Inset: Proposed wind farm
Detail: The Old Gaol

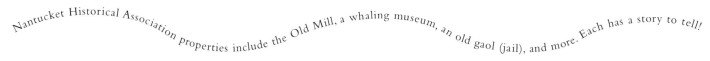

Nantucket Historical Association properties include the Old Mill, a whaling museum, an old gaol (jail), and more. Each has a story to tell!

Unique and Unspoiled, natural and unforgettable.

NANTUCKET HAS MANY HABITATS, including marshes, forests, dunes, ponds, and bogs. The Nantucket Conservation Foundation was formed in 1963 to protect these natural areas by buying and managing them. Starting with less than an acre, the foundation now includes 8,700 acres, covering 29 percent of the island. Thanks to these efforts and those of the Nantucket Land Bank, beautiful landscapes will be protected for future generations to enjoy.

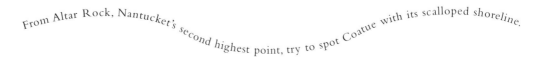

*From Altar Rock, Nantucket's second highest point, try to spot Coatue with its scalloped shoreline.*

**Main: Squam Farm**
**Inset: Coatue**
**Detail: Piping plover**

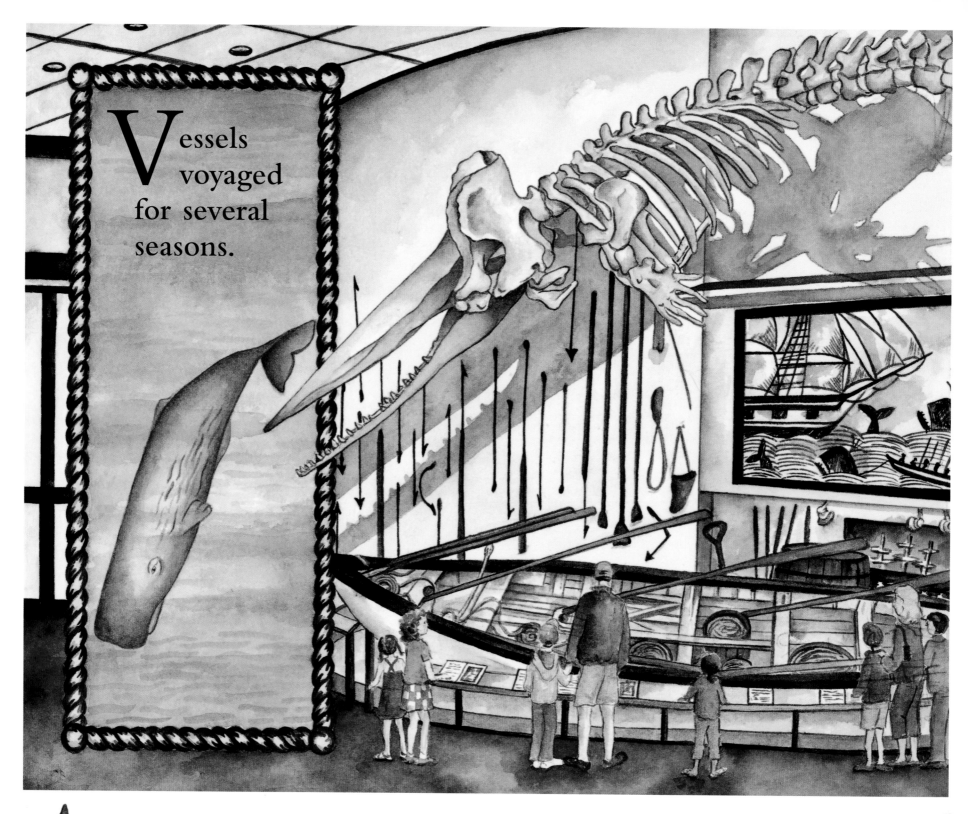

Vessels
voyaged
for several
seasons.

NANTUCKET WHALERS EQUIPPED THEIR SHIPS for voyages that often lasted several years. Life at sea ranged from monotonous to very dangerous. Herman Melville based his great novel *Moby Dick* on the tragic sinking of the Nantucket whale ship *Essex*. The dramatic 46-foot skeleton of a sperm whale that washed ashore in Sconset on New Year's Day 1998 is the centerpiece of the newly renovated Nantucket Whaling Museum.

Main: NHA Whaling Museum
Inset: Sperm whale
Detail: Nantucket sleigh ride

With the cry "Thar she blows!" small rowboats were sent out to harpoon the whale. Once hit, the whale took the crew on a wild "Nantucket sleigh ride."

**W**idow's walks weren't for worried women.

NANTUCKET'S ROOFWALKS are sometimes called "widow's walks," because some imagine wives anxiously awaiting their husbands' return from sea. But actually the walks were built so that sand could be poured down a burning chimney, and Nantucket women are known for their self-sufficient natures. In 1846, a fire broke out on Main Street that destroyed the downtown and wharf areas. For future protection, many structures were rebuilt using brick.

White marble squares set into brick sidewalks downtown mark the extent of the great fire.

Main: Roofwalks
Inset: Fire Hose Cart House
Detail: The great fire

E**X**citement
is here
as Xmas draws
near.

THE ANNUAL NANTUCKET STROLL, held on the first weekend in December, is part of the island's month-long holiday celebration, "Nantucket Noel." Visitors from all over the world arrive for festivities that include decorated shops, carolers dressed in old-fashioned clothes, and Santa, of course. He arrives by boat and rides up Main Street in a horse-drawn carriage.

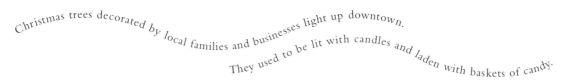

Christmas trees decorated by local families and businesses light up downtown.
They used to be lit with candles and laden with baskets of candy.

**Main:** Christmas Stroll, Main Street
**Inset:** Carolers
**Detail:** Happy holidays!

NANTUCKET RED

FROM CAPE COD TO NANTUCKET, the Figawi Race kicks off the sailing season. Sponsored by local yacht clubs, Race Week in August benefits the community sailing program. The island's safe harbor attracts boats of all sizes. Long ago, sailors crowded in the forecastle would have had a hard time imagining the amenities on today's luxury yachts boasting GPS systems, helicopters, and hot tubs. So much for scrimshaw!

The Rainbow Fleet parades around Brant Point in the Opera House Cup Regatta for classic wooden boats.

**Main: Rainbow Fleet, Brant Point**
**Inset: Nantucket Harbor**
**Detail: Opera House Cup**

**Z**innias and **Z**zucchini are trucked into town.

WITH LAND TOO SANDY FOR FARMING, Nantucket's first European settlers turned to raising sheep. With over fifteen thousand sheep on the island by 1800, the daunting task of shearing was turned into an annual festival. Following the decline of whaling, the Nantucket Agricultural Society was formed to support farmers and hosted annual fairs. Locally grown produce from Bartlett's two-hundred-year-old family farm is a summertime treat!

**Main:** Farm Truck, Main Street
**Inset:** Sheep shearing
**Detail:** Native fruits

Cranberries, blueberries, and Concord grapes are the only fruits native to the United States.

Double Dip

Egret

Flip flops

Inquirer & Mirror

Jeep

Nantucket flag

Oversand Vehicle Permit

Pail and shovel

Scallop

Turtle

Xmas

Yarn

Zschock

 *Arbor*

 *Bass*

 *Cranberry Scoop*

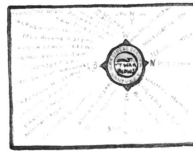 *Gardiner's Corner*

 *Hydrangea*

 *Kite*

 *Lobster*

 *Mermaid*

 *Quail*

 *Rosa Ragusa*

 *Umbrellas*

 *Victory*

*Weathervane*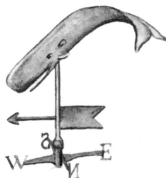